Farm Machines at Work

Harvesters
Go to Work

Jennifer Boothroyd

Lerner Publications ◆ Minneapolis

For Gavin

Lerner Publications Company
A division of Lerner Publishing Group, Inc.
241 First Avenue North
Minneapolis, MN 55401 USA

For reading levels and more information, look up this title at www.lernerbooks.com.

Main body text set in Billy Infant Semibold 17/23.
Typeface provided by SparkyType.

Library of Congress Cataloging-in-Publication Data

Names: Boothroyd, Jennifer, 1972– author.
Title: Harvesters go to work / Jennifer Boothroyd.
Description: Minneapolis : Lerner Publications, [2018] | Series: Farm machines at work | Audience: Ages 5-9. | Audience: K to grade 3. | Includes bibliographical references and index.
Identifiers: LCCN 2017056989 (print) | LCCN 2017048245 (ebook) | ISBN 9781541526075 (eb pdf) | ISBN 9781541526006 (lb : alk. paper) | ISBN 9781541527683 (pb : alk. paper)
Subjects: LCSH: Harvesting machinery—Juvenile literature. | Combines (Agricultural machinery)—Juvenile literature. | Harvesting—Juvenile literature.
Classification: LCC TJ1485 (print) | LCC TJ1485 .B66 2018 (ebook) | DDC 631.3/7—dc23

LC record available at https://lccn.loc.gov/2017056989

Manufactured in the United States of America
1-44568-35499-3/9/2018

TABLE OF CONTENTS

FARMS NEED
HARVESTERS

Harvesters are machines
that collect crops from fields.
Farmers use harvesters to
finish the job faster.

There are different harvesters for different kinds of crops. Grass harvesters cut grass with blades. A grape harvester gently shakes grapes off the vines.

This harvester helps farmers pick grapes.

Forage harvesters are usually smaller than other harvesters. They cut grass and other plants for forage. People feed forage crops to animals on the farm.

Combine harvesters are huge machines. They harvest grain crops like corn and wheat. Combines separate the tiny grains from the rest of the plant.

Combine harvesters are usually much bigger than forage harvesters.

Combines have very big engines. The combine needs a lot of power to run.

Take a peek under the combine's hood to see all that goes into making a combine run.

Buttons and switches inside the cab can control how fast a harvester is going.

A farmer controls a combine from the cab. There is a steering wheel in the cab. Buttons control parts of the machine.

The header at the front of a combine pushes cornstalks to the cutter. The cutter cuts the stalks. Then the machine knocks the corn kernels off the stalks.

The kernels collect in a grain tank at the bottom of the combine. The corncobs and stalks move out of the combine. These parts of the plants are called chaff.

Chaff can help keep the field healthy during winter.

Big fields can have enough corn to fill up many trailers with kernels.

An elevator brings corn kernels to a pipe called the unloading auger. The unloading auger pushes the kernels into a trailer that drives next to the combine.

Farmers use harvesters when the growing season is done. Most crops are picked once a season.

Farmers must work quickly to collect their crops. The crops will go bad if they are not picked soon enough.

Many kinds of corn and wheat are ready to harvest in the fall.

This farmer is using the lights on his harvester to see as it gets darker.

Many farmers work day and night to bring in the crops. Some harvesters have bright lights for working in the dark.

HARVESTERS YESTERDAY, TODAY, AND TOMORROW

In the past, crops were picked by hand or with small tools. It was hard and slow work.

A tool called a sickle helped farmers cut crops as they harvested.

People built machines to make the job easier. Horses pulled the machines.

Soon people used tractors to pull simple harvesters.

Today's harvesters are much faster than the machines from long ago. Farmers can pick crops quickly. New kinds of harvesters can also pick crops that farmers used to have to pick by hand.

Olive harvesters can collect olives without squishing the fruit.

In the future, harvesters will run on biofuel. This fuel is made from farm waste. Biofuel hurts Earth less than other fuels.

HARVESTER PARTS

cab

unloading auger

lights

steering wheel

header

tires

FUN HARVESTER FACTS

- It takes just seconds for grain to move through a combine.

- Some of the largest combines have 60-foot-wide (18 m) headers.

- Cyrus McCormick developed the first harvester in 1831. It was pulled by horses and would cut and catch grain.

GLOSSARY

biofuel: fuel made from waste

chaff: parts of a plant not eaten by people

combine: a harvester that cuts, collects, and separates the crop from the waste

crop: a plant grown to eat

forage: plants to feed farm animals

grain: plant seed used for food

growing season: the time of year when plants grow well

unloading auger: a pipe that empties grain from a combine

FURTHER READING

Bell, Samantha. *Combine Harvester.* Ann Arbor, MI: Cherry Lake, 2016.

Berne, Emma Carlson. *Balers Go to Work.* Minneapolis: Lerner Publications, 2019.

"Combine Harvester: Farm Machine Videos for Kids"
https://www.youtube.com/watch?v=jJRe-8rW6xs

Lindeen, Mary. *I Watch Fall Harvests.* Minneapolis: Lerner Publications, 2017.

Maimone, S. M. *Harvesters.* New York: Gareth Stevens, 2016.

New World Encyclopedia: Combine Harvester
http://www.newworldencyclopedia.org/entry/Combine_harvester

EXPLORE MORE

Learn even more about harvesters! Scan the QR code to see photos and videos of harvesters in action.

READ ALL THE BOOKS IN THE FARM MACHINES AT WORK SERIES!

Balers Go to Work

Cultivators Go to Work

Harvesters Go to Work

Skid Steers Go to Work

Sprayers Go to Work

Tractors Go to Work

INDEX

PHOTO ACKNOWLEDGMENTS

The images in this book are used with the permission of New Holland except: Sunny Forest/ Shutterstock.com, pp. 8 (background), 16 (background); Serg64/Shutterstock.com, p. 14; Hulton Deutsch/Corbis Historical/Getty Images, p. 16 (inset); Laura Westlund/Independent Picture Service, p. 23 (tractor). Design elements: enjoynz/DigitalVision Vectors/Getty Images; CHEMADAN/ Shutterstock.com; pingebat/Shutterstock.com; LongQuattro/Shutterstock.com.

Cover: New Holland.